I0791282

# Brain on Fear

Bridgett Ross

Copyright © 2019 Bridgett Ross

All rights reserved. No portion of this book may be reproduced in any form without permission from the publisher, except as permitted by U.S. copyright law.

Author photograph by Matt Ross

Although the author and publisher have made every effort to ensure that the information in this book was correct at press time, the author and publisher do not assume and hereby disclaim any liability to any party for any loss, damage, or disruption caused by errors or omissions, whether such errors or omissions result from negligence, accident, or any other cause.

This book is not intended as a substitute for the medical advice of physicians. The reader should regularly consult a physician in matters relating to his/her health and particularly with respect to any symptoms that may require diagnosis or medical attention.

Copyright © 2019 Bridgett Ross
All rights reserved.
ISBN: 9781688055261

To Emmitt,
may you name your fears
and tame them.

Did you know that fear is normal?
Did you also know that how you deal with fear affects your brain?

I was once afraid to pee.
Did I need to be?
No. But I was.

The day started with a cup of milk...

...and then I downed some juice...

...a tall glass of water...

...and a HUGE, steaming mug of hot cocoa.

You know what happens when you drink that much?!

I HAD TO PEE!

BAD!

Feeling as though I was about to explode,

I peered into the bathroom and thought,

*There is no way that toilet can hold all of my pee!*

I cried.

I wailed.

My mind screamed with terror:

"YOUR PEE WILL OVERFLOW THE TOILET!"

What was I to do?

Ask for help...
Pee my pants...
Pee outside...
Take a chance...
...and see if the toilet overflows.

I tiptoed cautiously to my dad and whispered,   "Daddy, I have to pee, but..."
I gulped. With tears in my eyes I confessed,   "...the toilet will overflow."
He could have responded a million different ways.

But he smiled and replied,   "Let me show you something."
He placed a bucket in the sink and turned on the faucet,
"Imagine that everyone you know is peeing in this bucket..."

Eventually, the entire bucket stood before me about to overflow. My dad asked,
"Would your pee fill this bucket?"
That was impossible! The bucket was gargantuan!
I giggled softly,  "noooooooooooooo."

We wobbled to the bathroom
hauling the big brimming bucket.

He slowly poured the pail of
pretend pee down the toilet.

The water whirled in a spiral
down as though the toilet had
been flushed.

That is when I learned...

# My pee cannot overflow the toilet!

I also learned a few other lessons. It's okay to feel afraid of silly things - even though fears usually don't feel silly at the time. It's okay to ask for help. If I had simply peed in the toilet, everything would have been okay. Lastly, even if the toilet had overflowed, it would not have been that bad.

All that learning shaped my brain! How?

First, the brain tells the body how to react to fear.

Like a house, the brain has an upstairs and downstairs.
The upstairs brain is the **thinking** brain.
The downstairs brain is the **feeling** brain.

Whenever we have strong emotions, the downstairs brain takes control.
That is why it seems like we cannot think straight
when we are really emotional.

When we feel threatened, our brains prepare the body to do whatever it takes to
survive, screaming commands like:


"RUN!"
"DON'T MOVE!"
"FIGHT!"


We pay no attention to the thinking brain
when we must focus on survival.

You are safe.
You can handle this.
I'm freaking out!!!
RUN!
Don't move!
FIGHT!

The fear response is left over from when we spent most of our time simply trying to survive.

Fear kickstarts an alarm system that tells our body to fight, flee, or freeze. Long ago, we regularly fought, fled, and froze to stay safe from danger.

While most humans face fewer threats than our ancient ancestors, our fear response is alive and well!

Sometimes, our downstairs brain thinks were are in danger when we are not and mislabels safe situations as threatening. The brain then alerts our body to enter survival mode without even checking with the upstairs brain!

So, when I felt a little nervous about peeing, my brain basically acted like I was facing a hungry tiger and declared:

Be still.
Pretend you're a
rock.

To deactivate
survival mode
you must:

1. Calm your body

2. Determine the actual danger

3. Decide what you can do

A calm body brings the thinking brain back online,
which then joins forces with the feeling brain
to help us understand things clearly.

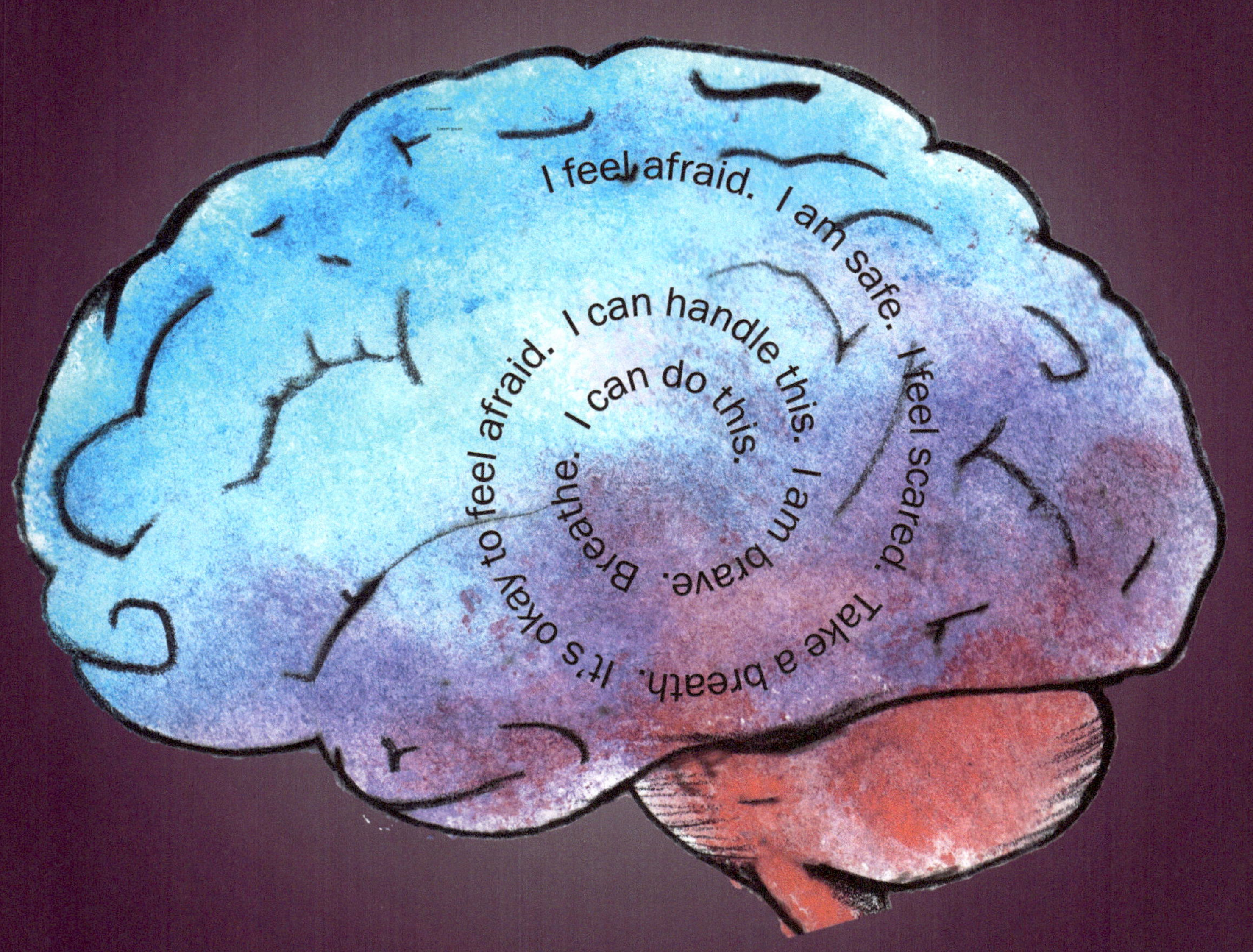

Now you know the basics about how fear is part of being human;
it is in our DNA.

The story of your brain on fear does not end there.

When we are born,
our brains are not completely developed.

The plan outlined by DNA is really just the beginning.

The things we do, choices we make, and people in our lives
determine how our brains develop.

Sad and scary experiences affect the brain one way.

Safe, positive, and loving experiences shape it another.

The Plan
"D.N.A."
• Brown eyes
• Curls tongue
• High energy
• Allergies
• Fight Flight Freeze!
• Human

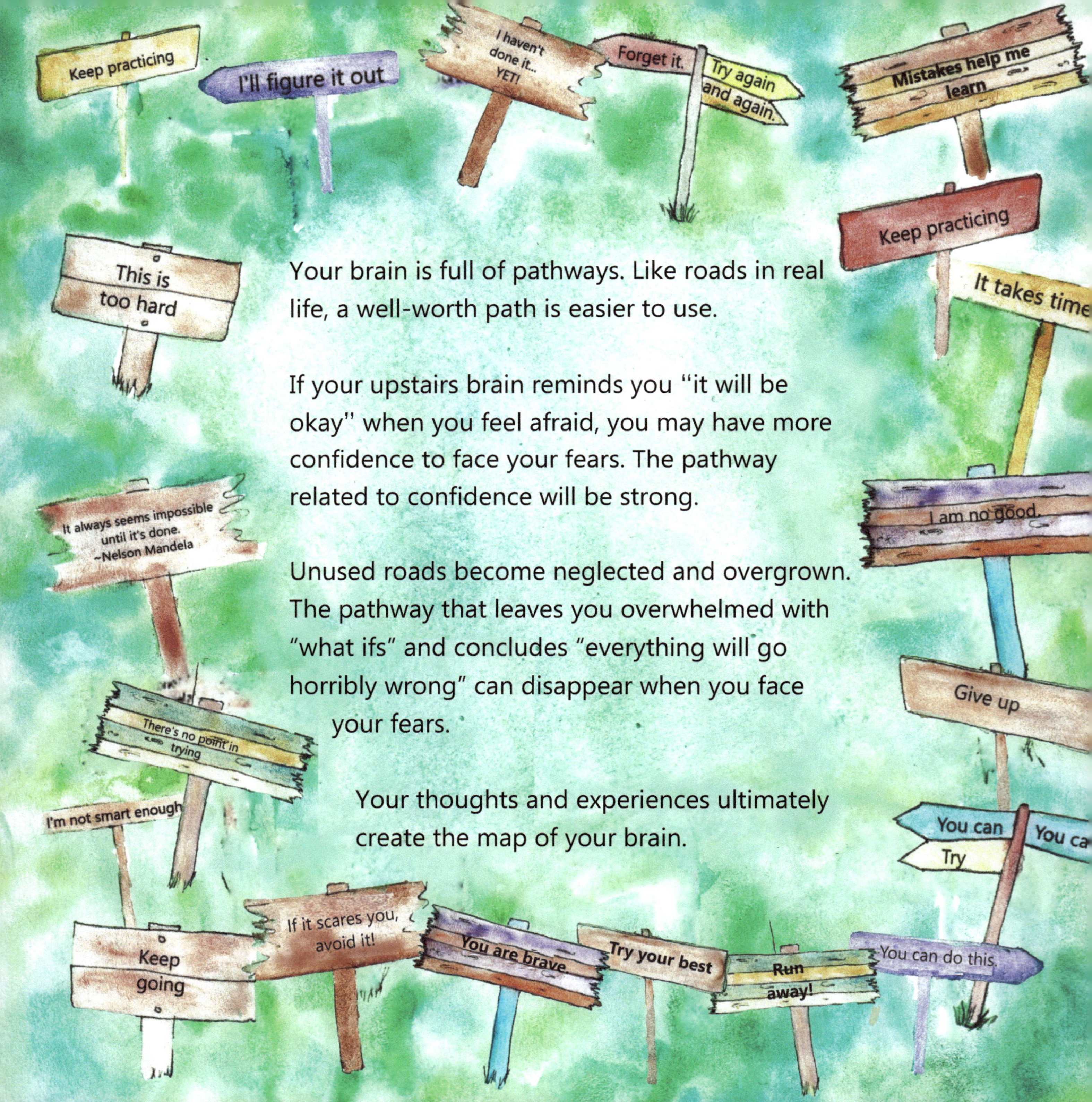


Your brain is full of pathways. Like roads in real life, a well-worth path is easier to use.

If your upstairs brain reminds you "it will be okay" when you feel afraid, you may have more confidence to face your fears. The pathway related to confidence will be strong.

Unused roads become neglected and overgrown. The pathway that leaves you overwhelmed with "what ifs" and concludes "everything will go horribly wrong" can disappear when you face your fears.

Your thoughts and experiences ultimately create the map of your brain.

(Even if something goes wrong)
It will be okay
Everything will go
HORRIBLY
WRONG!!!!

Avoidance affects your brain too.

If you avoid what you fear you'll believe,
"I CAN'T HANDLE IT!"

Your feeling brain may convince you things are
threatening when they are not.

Imagine what pathways would have developed if I had continued believing
I could overflow the toilet with my pee?

Unicorns?
Not to worry!
You can rewire your brain
no matter the fear.
Imagine that you
fear unicorns...
★ Electricians do not actually live in your brain.

Yes, unicorns. They are large muscular beasts and basically have swords on their heads.

Whenever you imagine unicorns, your feeling brain takes over. With pounding heart and sweaty palms, your brain screams, "You could never handle seeing a unicorn! Their horns are sharp and stabby!"

Just thinking of unicorns has your downstairs brain signaling "DANGER!'

You avoid EVERYTHING UNICORN.

You never give your downstairs brain a chance to calm down when imagining unicorns.

You never give your upstairs brain a chance to say, "Wait a minute! Unicorns are imaginary!"

That avoidance allows your brain to develop a well-worn path connecting unicorns to fear.

Then imagine one day, your teacher assigns a book featuring a unicorn.

At first, you might stare at the cover with trepidation. Then you might read each word with a pounding heart.

As you read the book, you may come to realize that, while unicorns are powerful beasts with sharp horns, they are more like knights than monsters.

If you give your brain time to calm down, you might accept that unicorns are imaginary. You might notice that stories usually depict unicorns as noble, dignified, gallant, and often magical.

By taking the time to engage with your fear, you would learn to think of unicorns differently. Then you would start to feel differently.

Your fear would change, and so would your brain.

Maybe thoughts of overflowing toilets and sharp, stabby unicorn horns don't leave you fearing for your life.

What about feeling afraid of the dark?

Or speaking in front of people?

Or certain animals?

What can you do to rewire your brain when you have these fears?

It is the same: You engage with your fear long enough for your feeling brain to calm down so that it can join forces with your thinking brain.

You may break down your fear into smaller steps.

It may take a lot of practice.

You may enlist the help of people who care about you.

No matter the fear, your actions can rewire your brain so that you feel differently.

Maybe it would help if I told you about my secret fear?

Sometimes I fear that I am not smart enough. Smart enough for what? Who really knows; it changes every day.

What I do know is that when I feel THIS fear, my thinking brain and feeling brain unite to work *against* me.

To conquer it, I have to make some difficult choices.

When I fear I am not smart enough to share my opinion or answer a question I...

SPEAK UP rather than STAY QUIET.

When people don't understand me, and I assume my intelligence is the problem, I...

STATE MY MESSAGE ANOTHER WAY

rather than  STOP TRYING.

When I believe not knowing something means I am not smart enough, I...

ASK A QUESTION (afterall, nobody knows everything)

rather than QUIETLY INSULT MYSELF FOR NOT KNOWING.

By taking the risk,
I give my brain a chance to realize that
while I might feel uncomfortable,

## I can handle it.

One
last
awesome
thing about
your brain is
that it can change
at any age.

So if you fear something for
80 years, you can face your
fear and still change your brain.

It will take more time and effort because
you are repairing and repaving roads that
have been overgrown for decades! So it is best
to get started now!

# In case you're curious…

- My dad really did alleviate my fears of overflowing the toilet by pretending my family members filled a giant bucket with pee!
- My use of "upstairs brain" and "downstairs brain" comes from Drs. Daniel Siegel and Tina Payne Bryson*
    - The technical term for "upstairs brain" is the prefrontal cortex (PFC)
    - The "downstairs brain" mostly focuses on the limbic system, and can include the brain stem
- While different parts of the brain control different things we do and feel, the brain is a complicated web of networks. Simple explanations usually don't tell the whole story, and much of the brain continues to remain a mystery.
- On the page featuring a tiger I focused on the "freeze" response because many people forget that "freeze" is just as much a survival instinct as fight and flight.
- A healthy brain is one in which the different parts of the brain work together well.
- There are many ways to manage fear, and effective ways usually wire the brain as described in this book.
- Scary life events and chronic stress have specific effects on your brain and health, for more information adults might want to read The Deepest Well by Dr. Nadine Burke Harris. **
- While healthy, safe, and loving environments early in life have the biggest impact on brain development, no matter your age you can change your brain – the term for this fact is neuroplasticity.
- The "rainbow brain" page shows many experiences that can affect brain development, but are not directly discussed in this book. It can help to look at those pictures and talk about what effects you think each of those experiences might have on the brain!

* The Whole Brain Child by Daniel Siegel and Tina Payne-Bryson
** The Deepest Well: Healing the Long-Term Effects of Childhood Adversity by Nadine Burke Harris

## About the Author

Bridgett Ross, PsyD is a psychologist and mom who lives in San Diego, CA. As a lover of the outdoors, she has faced many fears - a process that has been absolutely embarrassing at times, but always rewarding. She wrote *Brain on Fear* hoping that children and parents could learn more about how life experiences impact brain development, while also being entertained.

## Acknowledgments

Thank you to my husband and son for being patient me as I tinkered with this book, and generally being wonderful people who make my life better every day. Dad, thank you for teaching me that I cannot overflow the toilet with my pee, for your feedback on this book, and for accepting the abundance of hair on your illustration. I am grateful to Kirstin Filizetti for reading the first copy of this book and providing valuable feedback. Mrs. Penny's first grade class of 2018-19, thank you for letting me share an early copy of this book with you all. It helped me refine the content, and was awesome to hear you discuss your upstairs and downstairs brains.

www.ingramcontent.com/pod-product-compliance
Lightning Source LLC
Chambersburg PA
CBHW040203240726

48664CB00002B/817